RANJOT SINGH CHAHAL

Failure as a Learning Opportunity

First published by Rana Books (UK, India) 2023

Copyright © 2023 by Ranjot Singh Chahal

All rights reserved. No part of this publication may be reproduced, stored or transmitted in any form or by any means, electronic, mechanical, photocopying, recording, scanning, or otherwise without written permission from the publisher. It is illegal to copy this book, post it to a website, or distribute it by any other means without permission.

First edition

ISBN: 978-81-19786-14-5

Contents

1	Introduction	1
2	The Psychology of Learning and Memory	7
3	The Educational System and Learning Disabilities	13
4	Social Factors Affecting Learning	18
5	Embracing Failure as an Opportunity for Growth	24
6	Overcoming Obstacles to Learning	29
7	Learning Styles and Individual Differences	35
8	Learning for Lifelong Success	41

1

Introduction

1. Introduction: Understanding the Importance of Learning and the Consequences of Failure

Learning is a fundamental and continuous process that helps individuals acquire knowledge develop skills and adapt to new situations. It is an essential aspect of human growth and development enabling us to enhance our understanding make informed decisions and navigate the complexities of life.

When individuals fail to engage in learning or experience difficulties in the learning process it can have significant consequences that impact various aspects of their lives. Whether it relates to education career advancement personal growth or social interactions the failure to learn can limit opportunities and hinder progress. This article aims to delve deeper into the importance of learning and the far-reaching consequences that arise from the failure to learn.

1.1 Definition of Learning and its Significance

Learning can be defined as the process of acquiring knowledge skills attitudes or values through study experience or teaching. It involves a cognitive emotional and behavioral transformation that enables individuals to interpret and understand the world around them. Learning is not limited to classroom settings; it occurs throughout our lives encompassing formal education informal learning and experiential learning.

The significance of learning cannot be overstated. It forms the foundation of personal and professional development enabling individuals to adapt and thrive in a rapidly changing and interconnected world. Learning enhances critical thinking problem-solving abilities creativity and decision-making skills. It also plays a crucial role in fostering personal growth building self-confidence and fostering a sense of accomplishment and fulfillment.

In educational contexts learning is central to academic success. It equips students with the necessary knowledge skills and competencies to meet the challenges of their chosen fields of study. For professionals learning is essential for career advancement as it allows them to stay updated with industry trends acquire new skills and embrace innovation. From a societal perspective learning is vital for the progress and development of communities as it equips individuals with the tools to contribute to their respective fields and foster positive change.

1.2 Exploring the Negative Impact of Failure to Learn

When individuals fail to engage in the learning process or face significant difficulties in acquiring and applying knowledge and skills it can have profound consequences that extend beyond their immediate circumstances. These consequences encompass different areas of life including education career opportunities personal development and social interactions. Understanding these consequences sheds light on the far-reaching impact of the failure to learn.

a) Educational Consequences:

Failure to learn can have serious implications in educational settings. In schools and higher education institutions the primary purpose is to impart knowledge and facilitate learning. When students struggle to grasp concepts fail to acquire essential skills or lack motivation to engage in the learning process their academic performance suffers. Poor academic performance can lead to lower grades failure to graduate or an inability to pursue higher education opportunities.

Beyond academic consequences failure to learn can also impact students' self-esteem confidence and motivation. Students who consistently struggle with learning may develop negative attitudes towards education and perceive themselves as incapable of success. This mindset can create a vicious cycle as the lack of self-belief and motivation can further impede learning and academic performance.

b) Career Consequences:

Learning is crucial for career advancement and professional success. Individuals who fail to learn or neglect opportunities for skill development are more likely to face difficulties in the job market. In today's dynamic work environment where new technologies industries and job roles emerge rapidly individuals must be adaptable and continuously upskill themselves to remain competitive.

Without a commitment to learning and skill development individuals risk becoming obsolete or falling behind their peers. This lack of competitiveness can limit career growth opportunities result in stagnant wages or lead to unemployment. Additionally failure to learn may hinder individuals' ability to adapt to changes in their job roles or industries creating further career challenges.

c) Personal Development Consequences:

Learning plays a vital role in personal development shaping individuals' perspectives values and understanding of the world. When individuals fail to engage in learning or resist acquiring new knowledge they limit their personal growth potential. The failure to learn can hinder the development of critical thinking skills problem-solving abilities and creativity which are essential for personal and intellectual growth.

Furthermore individuals who do not actively pursue learning may miss out on opportunities to broaden their horizons expand their knowledge base and explore new interests. Learning enhances individuals' ability to understand diverse perspectives appreciate different cultures and engage critically with complex issues. The failure to learn can limit individuals' capacity for empathy creativity and adaptability hindering their personal growth and fulfillment.

d) Social Consequences:

Human interactions and social relationships are pervasive elements of our lives and learning plays a vital role in fostering positive social connections. Failure to learn can impact individuals' ability to effectively communicate collaborate and empathize with others. Inability or unwillingness to learn can lead to misunderstandings conflicts and strained relationships with family members friends colleagues or community members.

The failure to learn can also impede individuals' capacity to engage in civic activities contribute to community well-being and be informed and responsible citizens. Learning is essential for understanding social issues engaging in constructive dialogue and working towards collective solutions. Without a commitment to learning individuals may become disconnected from the social fabric leading to isolation marginalization or an inability to contribute meaningfully to their communities.

Overall the failure to learn can have far-reaching consequences that impact various aspects of an individual's life. From educational to career opportunities personal growth and social interactions the inability or reluctance to engage in learning can hinder progress limit opportunities and lead to broader personal and societal challenges.

To demonstrate the consequences of the failure to learn let's explore a few examples:

Example 1: Educational Consequences - Sarah a high school student consistently neglects her studies fails to attend classes regularly and lacks motivation to engage in learning activities. As a result her academic performance suffers leading to low grades and potential failure to graduate. Sarah's lack of commitment to learning hampers her chances of pursuing higher education opportunities or entering desired career paths.

2

The Psychology of Learning and Memory

2.1 Understanding How We Learn:

Learning is a complex psychological process that involves acquiring retaining and applying knowledge or skills. It is a fundamental aspect of human development and plays a critical role in our daily lives. Understanding how we learn can provide valuable insights into effective learning strategies and techniques.

One of the key theories in the psychology of learning is classical conditioning proposed by Ivan Pavlov. Classical conditioning is based on the idea that behaviors can be learned through repeated association between a stimulus and a response. Pavlov famously demonstrated this with his experiments on dogs where he conditioned them to salivate at the sound of a bell by repeatedly pairing the sound with the presentation of food.

Another important theory is operant conditioning introduced by

B.F. Skinner. Operant conditioning focuses on how behaviors are shaped through consequences or reinforcement. Skinner's experiments with rats in boxes (known as Skinner boxes) showed that behaviors that are reinforced are more likely to be repeated while behaviors that are punished or ignored are less likely to occur.

Cognitive psychology also plays a significant role in understanding how we learn. This perspective emphasizes the mental processes involved in learning such as attention perception memory and problem-solving. According to cognitive theorists like Jean Piaget and Lev Vygotsky learning involves actively constructing knowledge and understanding through processes like assimilation accommodation and scaffolding.

For example Piaget proposed that children go through stages of cognitive development where they gradually acquire new mental abilities and ways of thinking. This understanding of cognitive development has important implications for education as it suggests that teaching methods should be tailored to the developmental stage of the learner.

2.2 The Role of Memory in the Learning Process:

Memory is a crucial component of the learning process. It involves the encoding storage and retrieval of information. Without the ability to remember learning would be impossible as we would not be able to retain and apply new knowledge or skills.

There are several types of memory that play a role in learning.

Sensory memory is the initial stage of memory where information from the environment is briefly registered. It has a large capacity but a short duration. For example when you see a word on a page it is briefly stored in sensory memory before being transferred to short-term memory.

Short-term memory also known as working memory has limited capacity and duration. It is responsible for temporarily holding information in our conscious awareness. It is the memory system we use to keep information "online" while performing mental tasks. For instance when you solve a math problem mentally you hold the numbers in your short-term memory.

Long-term memory is the final stage of memory and has an almost unlimited capacity and potentially indefinite duration. It stores information for extended periods allowing for long-term retention and retrieval. Long-term memory can be further divided into explicit (declarative) and implicit (non-declarative) memory.

Explicit memory refers to conscious memory and it can be episodic (personal experiences) or semantic (general knowledge). For example recalling a specific event from your past or remembering the capital of a country relies on explicit memory.

Implicit memory involves the unconscious influence of past experiences on current behavior without conscious awareness. For instance riding a bike or typing on a keyboard are skills that have been learned and stored in implicit memory.

The role of memory in the learning process is multifaceted. The initial encoding of information into memory relies on attention and active engagement with the material. Without attention information is less likely to be encoded effectively into memory. Therefore creating an environment and learning tasks that enhance attention and engagement is crucial for learning.

Retention refers to the storage of information over time. The strength of memory traces can be influenced by various factors including the depth of processing emotional significance and repetition. For instance information that is deeply processed and connected to prior knowledge is more likely to be remembered than shallowly processed information.

Finally retrieval is the process of accessing information from memory. Effective retrieval is critical for applying knowledge or skills in the appropriate context. Retrieval cues such as cues present at the time of learning or specific associations can facilitate the retrieval process.

2.3 Factors Affecting Memory and Learning:

Various factors can influence memory and learning. Understanding these factors can help create optimal learning environments that enhance information retention and retrieval.

One important factor is attention. Attention is the process of focusing awareness on specific stimuli or tasks. When attention is directed towards information it increases the likelihood of encoding and retaining that information in memory. Distractions or divided attention can impair learning and memory processes.

Motivation is another critical factor. Motivation refers to the internal or external drives that energize and direct behavior. When individuals are motivated they are more likely to engage in learning activities and persist in the face of challenges. Motivation can be intrinsic (stemming from internal factors like interest or curiosity) or extrinsic (resulting from external factors like rewards or punishments).

Emotion also plays a significant role in memory and learning. Emotional experiences tend to be remembered more vividly and for longer periods. The amygdala a brain structure involved in emotional processing has connections with memory regions leading to enhanced memory consolidation and retrieval for emotionally charged events. However extreme emotional states can also impair attention and memory functioning.

The organization and structure of information can impact memory and learning as well. Meaningful and well-organized material is more easily encoded retained and retrieved. Strategies like chunking which involves grouping information into meaningful units can help enhance memory performance.

Repetition and practice are also essential for learning and memory. The mere exposure effect suggests that we tend to prefer stimuli that are familiar to us and repeated exposure can lead to enhanced memory and liking. Practice allows for the consolidation of learning strengthening neural connections and making information more accessible for retrieval.

Individual differences also affect memory and learning. Factors like intelligence prior knowledge and learning styles can impact how individuals acquire and retain information. Some individuals might excel at visual learning while others might prefer auditory or kinesthetic learning methods. Recognizing and accommodating these individual differences can optimize learning outcomes.

In conclusion the psychology of learning and memory provides valuable insights into the processes that underlie how we acquire retain and apply knowledge or skills. Understanding these processes can inform effective learning strategies and techniques that facilitate optimal learning outcomes. Factors such as attention motivation emotion organization repetition and individual differences all play a role in memory and learning. By considering these factors educators and learners can create environments and implement strategies that enhance learning and memory performance.

3

The Educational System and Learning Disabilities

3.1 Examining the Role of Schools in Facilitating Learning

The educational system plays a crucial role in facilitating learning and providing support to students with learning disabilities. Schools are responsible for creating an inclusive and supportive learning environment that accommodates the diverse needs of all students. In this section we will delve into the role of schools in facilitating learning and examine the challenges faced by students with learning disabilities.

Schools are expected to provide a quality education that meets the unique needs of every student including those with learning disabilities. They aim to promote academic social and emotional development ensuring that students are adequately prepared for future success. However for students with learning disabilities the traditional educational approach may not be sufficient to meet their individual needs.

Learning disabilities refer to a neurological condition that affects how individuals process store and communicate information. These disabilities can manifest in various areas including reading writing mathematics and language. Students with learning disabilities often struggle with tasks related to information processing memory and attention among others. As a result they may require additional support and interventions to optimize their learning experience.

3.2 Learning Disabilities and their Implications

Learning disabilities can present significant challenges to students' academic progress and overall well-being. These challenges can manifest in various ways impacting their self-esteem motivation and educational outcomes. Understanding the implications of learning disabilities is crucial for educators and policymakers to provide effective support to these students.

One of the most common learning disabilities is dyslexia which affects individuals' reading and language processing abilities. Students with dyslexia may have difficulty decoding words recognizing spelling patterns and comprehending written texts. This can hinder their academic progress and make learning frustrating and overwhelming.

Another prevalent learning disability is dyscalculia which affects mathematical abilities. Students with dyscalculia may struggle with basic arithmetic operations understanding mathematical concepts and solving mathematical problems. This can impact their overall math performance and limit their opportunities in fields that require strong numeracy skills.

Additionally there are language-based learning disabilities such as specific language impairment (SLI that affect individuals' oral and written communication skills. Students with SLI may experience challenges in understanding and expressing language making it difficult for them to participate actively in classroom discussions and engage with written assignments.

The presence of learning disabilities can significantly impact students' academic progress and emotional well-being. If not properly addressed these disabilities can lead to frustration low self-esteem and a lack of motivation to learn. Students with learning disabilities may be at a higher risk of experiencing academic failure social isolation and mental health issues compared to their peers without disabilities.

3.3 Strategies for Addressing Learning Disabilities

To ensure the success of students with learning disabilities schools must implement strategies and interventions that address their unique needs effectively. These strategies should focus on providing appropriate accommodations specialized instruction and support services to foster their academic and personal growth.

One key strategy is the implementation of Individualized Education Programs (IEPs) or 504 Plans. These are legally mandated documents that outline the specific accommodations and support services that students with learning disabilities require. IEPs are developed collaboratively with the student parents teachers and other relevant professionals ensuring that the student's individual needs are met.

Accommodations may include modifications to the learning environment such as preferential seating additional time for tests and the use of assistive technology. These accommodations aim to level the playing field for students with learning disabilities and enable them to participate actively in the classroom.

Specialized instruction is another crucial component in addressing learning disabilities. This may involve the provision of remedial support in areas of difficulty such as reading or math. For example students with dyslexia may benefit from explicit phonics instruction or multisensory reading programs that cater to their specific learning needs.

Collaboration between teachers special education professionals and related service providers is essential in delivering effective instruction and support. This collaboration ensures that the strategies employed are evidence-based and align with the individualized needs of the student. Regular communication and progress monitoring help to identify areas of improvement and adjust interventions accordingly.

In addition to academic support addressing the emotional well-being of students with learning disabilities is equally important. Schools can provide counseling services social skills training and peer support programs to help students build resilience self-confidence and positive self-image. Creating a safe and inclusive school culture that promotes acceptance and understanding can also contribute to the overall well-being of students with learning disabilities.

Furthermore providing professional development opportunities for teachers is crucial in ensuring that they are equipped with the knowledge and skills to support students with learning disabilities effectively. Training should focus on understanding different learning disabilities implementing evidence-based instructional strategies and utilizing assistive technologies. By enhancing teachers' expertise schools can foster an inclusive learning environment that supports the success of all students.

In conclusion schools play a vital role in facilitating learning for students with learning disabilities. By recognizing the implications of learning disabilities and implementing appropriate strategies and interventions schools can create an inclusive environment where all students can thrive. Addressing the needs of students with learning disabilities requires collaborative efforts involving teachers parents and other professionals ensuring that individualized support and accommodations are provided. Ultimately by embracing the diversity of learners and tailoring instruction to their needs schools can empower students with learning disabilities to reach their full potential.

4

Social Factors Affecting Learning

Learning is influenced by a variety of social factors that can facilitate or hinder the learning process. These factors include peer pressure cultural and societal barriers and the overall social environment in which learning takes place. In this section we will delve into these social factors and discuss their impact on learning.

4.1 The Influence of Peer Pressure on Learning

Peer pressure is a powerful social force that can significantly impact an individual's learning experience. Peer pressure refers to the influence exerted by peers on an individual to conform to their attitudes behaviors and values. It can be both positive and negative depending on the context.

Positive peer pressure can be motivating and encourage students to excel academically. For example if students observe their peers studying diligently or scoring well on exams they may feel motivated to do the same in order to fit in or meet the expectations of their peer group. This positive influence can create a healthy competitive environment that fosters learning and academic growth.

On the other hand negative peer pressure can have detrimental effects on learning. Peer pressure to engage in risky or counterproductive behaviors such as skipping classes using drugs or engaging in cheating can divert students' attention away from their studies and hinder their learning progress. Students may feel compelled to conform to the norms of their peer group even if those norms are not conducive to academic success.

To illustrate the impact of peer pressure on learning let's consider an example. Suppose a high school student is part of a peer group where it is considered "cool" to underperform academically and engage in disruptive behavior. This student may feel pressured to conform to this group's expectations and may neglect their studies resulting in poor academic performance. In this case the negative influence of peer pressure impedes the student's ability to learn effectively.

Educators and parents play a crucial role in counteracting negative peer pressure and promoting a positive learning environment. By fostering a supportive and inclusive classroom climate teachers can encourage respectful interaction among students and discourage the acceptance of negative influences. Parents can also instill values and provide guidance that promotes a strong sense of self-confidence and independence in their children enabling them to resist negative peer pressure.

4.2 Cultural and Societal Barriers to Learning

Cultural and societal barriers encompass a range of factors that can hinder learning for individuals from different backgrounds and cultures. These barriers can include language barriers prejudice and discrimination socioeconomic disparities and cultural expectations and values.

Language barriers can have a profound impact on learning particularly for students who come from non-English-speaking backgrounds. When students are not proficient in the language of instruction they may struggle to understand concepts express themselves and fully engage in classroom activities. This language barrier can lead to feelings of frustration and alienation making it difficult for these students to fully participate and learn effectively.

Prejudice and discrimination can also create barriers to learning. Students who belong to minority groups may face bias and stereotyping which can undermine their self-esteem and confidence. This negative social environment can create a hostile learning environment and hinder their ability to focus on learning.

Socioeconomic disparities can significantly affect learning opportunities. Students from economically disadvantaged backgrounds may lack access to educational resources such as textbooks technology and extracurricular activities. They may also face challenges related to housing instability food insecurity and limited parental support. These external factors can impede their ability to fully engage in their studies and reach their full learning potential.

Cultural expectations and values can also pose barriers to learning. Different cultures may place varying emphasis on education and have different expectations regarding appropriate career paths and goals. For example in some cultures there may be a stronger emphasis on practical skills or vocational training rather than academic pursuits. Additionally cultural norms surrounding gender roles may limit educational opportunities for girls or discourage certain fields of study. These cultural expectations can shape individuals' aspirations and choices potentially limiting their access to certain educational opportunities.

To address these cultural and societal barriers educational institutions need to adopt inclusive practices that value diversity and promote equal access to quality education. This includes providing language support for students who are non-native speakers implementing anti-bullying policies offering financial assistance programs for students from economically disadvantaged backgrounds and creating a culturally responsive curriculum that respects and reflects the diverse backgrounds of students.

4.3 Addressing Social Factors to Enhance Learning

To enhance learning it is essential to address the social factors that can either facilitate or hinder the learning process. Here are some strategies that can be implemented to create a supportive and conducive social environment:

1. Foster Positive Relationships: Encouraging positive relationships among students as well as between students and teachers can create a sense of belonging and support. This can be achieved through team-building activities collaborative learning opportunities and open communication channels.

2. Promote Peer Tutoring: Peer tutoring programs can leverage the power of positive peer influence. Pairing students who excel in a particular subject with those who are struggling can not only provide academic support but also instill a sense of responsibility and cooperation.

3. Cultivate an Inclusive Classroom Climate: Teachers should create an inclusive classroom environment that appreciates and values diversity. This involves promoting respect empathy and understanding among students. Teachers can incorporate multicultural perspectives into the curriculum and provide opportunities for students to share and learn about each other's cultures.

4. Provide Language Support: For students facing language barriers offering language support services such as English as a Second Language (ESL) programs or bilingual instruction can help bridge the communication gap and enable them to fully participate in classroom activities.

5. Implement Anti-Bullying Policies: Schools should have clear anti-bullying policies and procedures to address any instances of bullying or discrimination. This helps create a safe and respectful learning environment where students feel valued and protected.

6. Address Socioeconomic Disparities: Educational institutions should offer support services to students from economically disadvantaged backgrounds. This can include providing free or reduced-price meals offering tutoring or mentoring programs and making resources such as textbooks and technology accessible to all students.

7. Encourage Parental Involvement: Engaging parents and caregivers in their children's education can have a significant positive impact on learning. Schools can promote parental involvement through regular communication parent-teacher conferences and workshops that equip parents with strategies to support their children's learning at home.

Addressing social factors to enhance learning requires a multifaceted approach involving educators parents policymakers and communities. By recognizing and addressing the social factors that influence learning we can create a more equitable and inclusive educational system that empowers all learners to reach their full potential.

5

Embracing Failure as an Opportunity for Growth

Failure is a natural part of life and the learning process. Instead of viewing failure as something negative we can choose to embrace it as an opportunity for growth and improvement. By reframing failure and shifting our perspective we can leverage our mistakes and setbacks to become better versions of ourselves.

One key aspect of embracing failure is realizing that failure is not the end result but rather a stepping stone on the path to success. Thomas Edison the inventor of the light bulb famously said "I have not failed. I've just found 10000 ways that won't work." Edison's attitude exemplifies the mindset required to embrace failure. Each failure presents an opportunity to learn valuable lessons and gain insights that can lead to future success.

When we view failure as a learning opportunity we are more likely to take risks step out of our comfort zones and push ourselves beyond our limits. By embracing failure we cultivate resilience perseverance and a growth mindset. These qualities are essential for personal and professional development.

Moreover failure provides us with critical feedback about our abilities strategies and decision-making processes. It highlights areas where we need to improve and helps us identify the necessary adjustments for future endeavors. Without failure it can be difficult to assess our progress and make the necessary course corrections.

To illustrate the power of embracing failure let's consider the example of a new entrepreneur starting a business. Initially they may encounter numerous setbacks and failures. Perhaps their first product fails to gain traction in the market or they experience financial difficulties. Instead of giving up the entrepreneur embraces these failures as learning opportunities. They analyze what went wrong identify areas for improvement and adjust their strategies accordingly. With each setback they gain valuable insights about their target market product development marketing techniques and financial management. As a result they become more resilient knowledgeable and adaptable increasing their chances of success in future entrepreneurial endeavors.

5.2 Techniques for Effective Reflection and Learning from Failure

Reflection is a vital component of the learning process particularly when it comes to learning from failure. It involves intentionally examining our experiences actions and outcomes to gain deeper insights and understanding. Effective reflection allows us to extract valuable lessons from failure and apply them to future situations. In this section we will explore some techniques that can facilitate effective reflection and learning from failure.

1. Self-Reflection: Taking the time to reflect on our failures is crucial. This involves asking ourselves tough questions such as: What worked well? What went wrong? What could I have done differently? What lessons can I learn from this experience? By engaging in honest self-reflection we can gain a deeper understanding of our strengths weaknesses and areas for improvement.

2. Seeking Feedback: In addition to self-reflection seeking feedback from others can provide valuable perspectives. Feedback from mentors colleagues or trusted individuals can help us gain insights and identify blind spots that we may not have considered. Constructive feedback offers alternative viewpoints and can help us identify areas where we need to make adjustments.

3. Keeping a Failure Journal: Maintaining a journal specifically dedicated to documenting our failures can be a powerful tool for learning. In this journal we can write about our experiences emotions and key takeaways from each failure. By recording our failures in detail we can track patterns identify recurring mistakes and monitor our growth over time.

4. Analyzing Root Causes: When faced with failure it is essential to analyze the root causes behind our shortcomings. This involves digging deep to identify underlying factors contributing to the failure. By understanding the root causes we can

implement more targeted solutions and prevent the recurrence of similar failures in the future.

5. Applying the "Five Whys" Technique: The "Five Whys" technique is a problem-solving approach that involves asking "why" five times to uncover the root cause of a problem. By asking "why" successively we can delve deeper into the underlying issues until we reach the core reason behind the failure. This technique helps us uncover hidden factors and promotes a more comprehensive understanding of the failure.

6. Experimentation and Iteration: Learning from failure involves a process of experimentation and iteration. After identifying the lessons learned it is crucial to apply those lessons and adjust our strategies accordingly. By continuously experimenting and iterating we can refine our approaches and increase our chances of success in future endeavors.

To illustrate these techniques further let's consider the example of a student who fails a final exam. Through self-reflection the student may realize that they didn't allocate enough time for studying were overwhelmed with other commitments and lacked effective study strategies. Seeking feedback from the professor may reveal additional insights such as areas where their understanding was lacking or misunderstanding of certain concepts. By keeping a failure journal the student can document their thoughts and emotions about the failure as well as any patterns they notice in their study habits. Analyzing the root causes may reveal deeper issues such as poor time management skills or difficulties comprehending specific topics. By applying the "Five Whys" technique the student may discover that their poor time management skills stem from a lack of prioritization and organizational skills. Armed with these insights the student can experiment with new study techniques improve their time management skills and seek additional support to rectify their shortcomings.

In conclusion learning from failure requires embracing failure as an opportunity for growth and using reflection as a tool to extract valuable lessons. By reframing failure we can shift our perspective and view setbacks as stepping stones to success. Through self-reflection seeking feedback journaling analyzing root causes and applying problem-solving techniques we can gain deeper insights and understanding of our failures. Learning from failure is a powerful process that builds resilience cultivates a growth mindset and enhances our chances of success in future endeavors.

6

Overcoming Obstacles to Learning

Learning is a fundamental aspect of human development and growth. It allows us to acquire new knowledge develop new skills and expand our understanding of the world. However there are often obstacles that can hinder the learning process. In this section we will explore three common obstacles to learning: procrastination perfectionism and lack of motivation and discuss strategies for overcoming them.

6.1 Procrastination and its Negative Impact on Learning:

Procrastination is the act of delaying or postponing tasks. It is a common obstacle to learning that many people experience. When we procrastinate we put off important tasks or learning activities until the last minute which can have detrimental effects on our ability to learn effectively.

One of the reasons people procrastinate is the feeling of being overwhelmed or having a lack of confidence in their ability to complete a task. For example a student might procrastinate on studying for a test because they feel overwhelmed by the amount of material they need to cover. Another common reason for procrastination is the desire for immediate gratification. Instead of focusing on long-term benefits such as gaining knowledge or improving skills we are drawn to short-term rewards or distractions.

Procrastination has a negative impact on learning because it limits the amount of time and effort we can dedicate to learning. When we procrastinate we have less time for deep learning and understanding and we often resort to shallow learning or cramming. This can result in lower-quality learning outcomes and a limited retention of knowledge over time.

To overcome procrastination it is important to be aware of its underlying causes and implement strategies to counteract them. One effective strategy is to break down tasks into smaller more manageable chunks. By dividing a large task into smaller bite-sized pieces it becomes less overwhelming and more achievable. This allows us to make progress incrementally and reduces the chances of procrastination.

Another strategy is to create a schedule or set specific deadlines for each task. By assigning specific time slots for learning activities we can hold ourselves accountable and eliminate the tendency to postpone tasks indefinitely. Additionally setting realistic goals and rewarding ourselves upon completion can provide motivation and help combat the desire for immediate gratification.

Furthermore it is important to identify and address any underlying fear or anxiety that may be contributing to procrastination. Understanding the roots of our fears can help us develop strategies to manage them effectively. Techniques such as mindfulness stress management exercises and seeking support from others can assist in reducing anxiety and increasing focus and productivity.

6.2 Dealing with Perfectionism and Fear of Failure:

Perfectionism is another obstacle that can hinder the learning process. It is the belief that one must achieve flawless results in all tasks and activities. Perfectionists often set unrealistically high standards for themselves leading to a fear of failure and a reluctance to take risks or try new things.

Perfectionism can be especially detrimental to learning because it creates an environment of constant self-judgment and criticism. When we strive for perfection we become preoccupied with avoiding mistakes rather than focusing on the process of learning and growth. As a result we may avoid challenging tasks that could potentially lead to failure limiting our ability to learn and develop new skills.

To overcome perfectionism it is important to reframe our mindset and adopt a more growth-oriented approach to learning. Instead of focusing solely on the end result we should shift our attention to the process and the journey of acquiring knowledge and skills. Embracing a growth mindset means recognizing that failure and mistakes are inevitable and essential steps in the learning process.

One effective strategy to combat perfectionism is setting realistic expectations and goals. By setting attainable objectives we can reduce the pressure to achieve perfection and allow ourselves the space to learn and make mistakes. It is important to celebrate small victories along the way and recognize that progress is more important than perfection.

Another strategy is to seek feedback and constructive criticism from others. By engaging in peer review seeking mentorship or participating in group discussions we can gain different perspectives and valuable insights into our learning process. Constructive feedback can help us identify areas of improvement and provide guidance for further development.

Additionally practicing self-compassion is crucial in overcoming perfectionism. We must learn to treat ourselves with kindness and understanding when we make mistakes or encounter challenges. Being gentle with ourselves and acknowledging our efforts rather than being overly critical can help us develop resilience and maintain motivation in the face of setbacks.

6.3 Enhancing Motivation and Self-Discipline:

Motivation and self-discipline are essential for effective learning. However it is common to experience periods of low motivation or difficulty in staying disciplined especially when faced with challenging or tedious learning tasks. In this section we will explore strategies for enhancing motivation and self-discipline to overcome this obstacle.

One way to enhance motivation is to connect the learning

material to personal interests and goals. When we can see the relevance and importance of what we are learning we are more likely to feel motivated to engage with the material. For example if a student is interested in pursuing a career in medicine they may be more motivated to learn biology and chemistry because they understand the direct link to their future goals.

Another strategy is to break down long-term goals into smaller more achievable milestones. By setting short-term objectives that align with the overall learning goals we can maintain a sense of progress and accomplishment along the way. This helps to sustain motivation and provides a clear path to follow.

Additionally utilizing different learning strategies and techniques can keep the learning process exciting and engaging. Experimenting with various methods such as visual aids hands-on activities group discussions or online resources can help prevent monotony and make learning more enjoyable. By incorporating variety into our learning routine we can sustain motivation and avoid boredom.

Developing self-discipline is also crucial for effective learning. It involves setting priorities managing time effectively and resisting distractions or temptations. One helpful strategy is to create a conducive learning environment that minimizes distractions. This may involve finding a quiet space turning off notifications on electronic devices or using productivity tools to stay focused.

Setting specific goals and establishing a routine can also enhance self-discipline. By determining specific tasks to be accomplished within designated time frames we can hold ourselves accountable and ensure consistent progress. Breaking down tasks into smaller manageable parts and using time-blocking techniques can be effective in managing time and staying disciplined.

Furthermore finding sources of external accountability can be beneficial. This may involve studying with a study group or finding an accountability partner who can hold us responsible for completing tasks and meeting deadlines. Sharing progress discussing challenges and celebrating achievements with others can provide motivation and promote self-discipline.

In conclusion overcoming obstacles to learning is crucial for effective and meaningful learning experiences. Procrastination perfectionism and lack of motivation can all hinder the learning process. However by implementing strategies such as breaking tasks into smaller portions setting realistic goals reframing our mindset seeking feedback connecting learning to personal interests and developing self-discipline we can overcome these obstacles and foster a more productive and enjoyable learning journey. Remember learning is a lifelong process and it is through overcoming obstacles that we grow and develop as individuals.

7

Learning Styles and Individual Differences

In the field of education it is widely recognized that individuals have diverse learning styles and preferences. Learning styles refer to the different ways in which individuals perceive process and retain information. These styles can be categorized into visual auditory and kinesthetic learning styles.

7.1 Visual Auditory and Kinesthetic Learning Styles

Visual learners rely on visual aids such as images diagrams charts and videos to understand and remember information. They have a preference for seeing information presented in a clear and organized manner. Visual learners tend to benefit from techniques such as using visual cues creating visual representations and utilizing colors and symbols to aid their learning. For example a visual learner may find it helpful to use mind maps or flowcharts to visually organize concepts.

Auditory learners on the other hand learn best through listening and speaking. They prefer to hear information and understand it by engaging in discussions lectures and verbal explanations. Auditory learners often have good listening skills and a strong ability to remember spoken information. Strategies that cater to their learning style include participating in group discussions using audio recordings or podcasts and reciting or discussing information aloud. For instance an auditory learner may benefit from recording lectures or reading aloud to themselves.

Kinesthetic learners also known as tactile learners learn best through physical activities and hands-on experiences. They have a preference for movement and interaction and they tend to learn and remember information better when they can engage multiple senses. Kinesthetic learners benefit from activities such as experiments role-playing simulations and interactive games. For example a kinesthetic learner may find it helpful to use manipulative tools or physical models to understand abstract concepts.

It is important to note that while individuals may have a dominant learning style they are not limited to that style alone. Many people exhibit a combination of learning styles with one style being more predominant than others. Additionally learning styles can vary depending on the subject matter or the context in which learning takes place. Therefore it is essential to consider individual differences and adapt instructional strategies accordingly.

7.2 Catering to Different Learning Preferences

To effectively cater to different learning preferences educators need to employ a variety of instructional methods and learning activities. By incorporating multiple modalities into their teaching they can engage a wider range of learners and create a more inclusive learning environment. Here are some strategies for catering to visual auditory and kinesthetic learners:

Visual learners:
1. Use visual aids such as slides diagrams and charts during lectures and presentations.
2. Provide handouts or notes with visual representations of key information.
3. Encourage visual learners to take notes and create visual summaries of concepts.
4. Incorporate videos animations and images to illustrate and reinforce important concepts.
5. Use color coding and highlighting to emphasize important points.

Auditory learners:
1. Deliver information through oral presentations lectures and discussions.
2. Provide opportunities for auditory learners to discuss and debate concepts with their peers.
3. Use audio recordings or podcasts as supplementary resources for auditory learners to review.
4. Encourage auditory learners to read aloud or summarize information in their own words.
5. Incorporate music or sound effects to enhance learning experiences.

Kinesthetic learners:

1. Incorporate hands-on activities experiments and simulations into lessons.

2. Provide opportunities for kinesthetic learners to manipulate objects or materials while learning.

3. Encourage role-playing or acting out scenarios related to the subject matter.

4. Organize field trips or outdoor activities that allow kinesthetic learners to interact with their surroundings.

5. Use physical movement such as gestures or body actions to reinforce learning.

By utilizing a combination of these strategies educators can provide different learning opportunities and facilitate meaningful learning experiences for students with diverse learning preferences.

7.3 Capitalizing on Individual Strengths for Effective Learning

In addition to understanding and catering to different learning styles it is also important to recognize and capitalize on individual strengths and talents for effective learning. Each individual brings unique skills interests and ways of thinking to the learning process. By acknowledging and leveraging these individual strengths educators can help students thrive academically and personally.

One way to capitalize on individual strengths is through differentiated instruction. This approach involves tailoring instruction to match the abilities interests and learning preferences of each student. By providing a variety of learning options and flexible assessments educators can accommodate different learning styles and allow students to demonstrate their knowledge and understanding in ways that showcase their strengths. For example a student with a talent for visual arts could be given the opportunity to create a visual representation or graphic organizer to demonstrate their understanding of a concept.

Another way to capitalize on individual strengths is by fostering a positive and supportive learning environment. This includes creating opportunities for students to showcase their strengths and talents providing constructive feedback and encouragement and promoting a growth mindset. When students feel valued and supported they are more likely to take risks engage actively in learning and develop confidence in their abilities.

Furthermore incorporating real-world connections and applications in the learning process can help students see the relevance and importance of what they are learning. By linking academic concepts to real-life situations examples and problem-solving scenarios educators can tap into students' interests and motivations making the learning experience more meaningful and engaging.

In conclusion understanding learning styles and individual differences is crucial for effective teaching and learning. By recognizing the visual auditory and kinesthetic learning styles educators can employ a variety of instructional strategies to cater to diverse learning preferences. Additionally by capitalizing on individual strengths and creating a supportive learning environment educators can empower students to reach their full potential. By valuing and catering to the unique needs and abilities of each student educators can create an inclusive educational experience that fosters growth engagement and achievement.

8

Learning for Lifelong Success

In today's fast-paced and ever-changing world learning has become an essential skill for lifelong success. Continuous learning is no longer just a choice; it has become a necessity for individuals to adapt grow and thrive in both personal and professional spheres. In this section we will explore the concept of cultivating a growth mindset strategies for continuous learning and personal development and the importance of overcoming setbacks and embracing a resilient learning process.

8.1 Cultivating a Growth Mindset

The first step towards achieving lifelong success through learning is to cultivate a growth mindset. Coined by psychologist Carol Dweck a growth mindset refers to the belief that one's abilities and intelligence can be developed with effort practice and dedication. In contrast a fixed mindset assumes that skills and traits are inherent and unchangeable.

People with a growth mindset embrace challenges view failures as opportunities for learning and persevere in the face of obstacles. They believe that their abilities can be improved through hard work and learning from mistakes. In contrast those with a fixed mindset tend to avoid challenges fear failure and give up easily when faced with difficulties.

Cultivating a growth mindset involves a shift in perception and adopting certain attitudes and behaviors. Some strategies to develop a growth mindset include:

1. Embrace challenges: Seek out opportunities that push you outside your comfort zone. By tackling challenging tasks you can develop new skills and abilities.

Example: A programmer who wants to improve their coding skills takes on complex coding projects that require extensive research and problem-solving. This challenge helps them expand their knowledge and become a better programmer.

2. Emphasize effort and persistence: Focus on the process rather than the end result. Recognize the value of effort and perseverance in achieving success.

Example: An athlete who wants to improve their running speed sets a training schedule and sticks to it even during difficult training sessions. They understand that consistent effort and persistence are crucial for enhancing their performance.

3. Embrace failures as learning opportunities: Instead of seeing failure as a reflection of one's abilities view it as a chance to grow and improve. Analyze the reasons for failure learn from

mistakes and make necessary adjustments.

Example: An entrepreneur whose business venture failed critically examines the reasons behind the failure learns from the experience and applies the lessons to their next entrepreneurial endeavor. This failure becomes a valuable learning opportunity.

4. Foster a love for learning: Develop a passion for acquiring knowledge expanding skills and seeking new experiences. Embrace a lifelong curiosity and thirst for learning.

Example: A writer who wants to improve their storytelling skills reads books from various genres attends writing workshops and explores different writing techniques to enhance their craft.

By cultivating a growth mindset individuals are more likely to approach learning with enthusiasm and resilience. This mindset fosters a belief in the power of continuous learning and personal development.

8.2 Strategies for Continuous Learning and Personal Development

Once a growth mindset is established the next step is to adopt strategies for continuous learning and personal development. Continuous learning involves acquiring new knowledge developing skills and expanding one's understanding throughout life. Personal development on the other hand focuses on nurturing personal qualities values and motivations to enhance overall well-being and success.

Here are some strategies for continuous learning and personal development:

1. Set clear goals: Define your learning objectives and determine what you want to achieve. Having clear goals provides a sense of direction and motivates you to pursue learning opportunities.

Example: A graphic designer wants to learn web design. They set a goal to learn HTML CSS and Javascript within six months to enhance their skills and secure better job opportunities.

2. Create a learning plan: Develop a structured plan outlining what skills and knowledge you want to acquire how you will learn them and a timeline for achieving your learning goals.

Example: A business professional interested in leadership development creates a learning plan that includes taking leadership courses attending conferences reading leadership books and seeking mentorship from experienced leaders.

3. Utilize diverse learning methods: Explore different learning resources and methods to find what works best for you. This can include online courses books podcasts workshops mentoring or experiential learning.

Example: A language enthusiast who wants to learn Spanish uses a combination of language-learning apps online courses conversational practice with native speakers and immersion experiences to accelerate their learning process.

4. Seek feedback and reflection: Regularly seek feedback from

mentors peers or experts in your field. Reflection allows you to identify areas for improvement and reinforce learning.

Example: A teacher attending a professional development workshop seeks feedback from colleagues on their teaching strategies. They reflect on the feedback and make necessary adjustments to enhance their teaching effectiveness.

5. Foster a learning community: Surround yourself with like-minded individuals who value learning and personal growth. Engage in discussions share knowledge and collaborate to enhance the learning experience.

Example: A group of entrepreneurs forms a mastermind group where they meet regularly to discuss business challenges share insights and provide support and accountability to each other. This community fosters continuous learning and personal development.

6. Embrace technology and innovation: Leverage technological advancements such as online platforms e-learning tools and digital resources to access learning opportunities conveniently and stay updated with the latest information in your field.

Example: A healthcare professional uses virtual reality simulations to enhance their surgical skills and stay abreast of new surgical techniques and technologies.

By incorporating these strategies into your learning journey you can maintain a commitment to continuous learning and personal development paving the way for lifelong success.

8.3 Overcoming Setbacks and Embracing a Resilient Learning Process

In the pursuit of lifelong success and continuous learning setbacks and obstacles are inevitable. However what sets successful learners apart is their ability to overcome setbacks and embrace a resilient learning process.

Resilience refers to the ability to bounce back from adversity adapt to change and remain persistent in the face of challenges. It enables individuals to persevere learn from setbacks and continue their learning journey. Here are some strategies to overcome setbacks and foster a resilient learning process:

1. Embrace a growth mindset towards failure: See failure as a stepping stone towards success rather than a roadblock. Adopt a positive perspective focusing on the lessons learned and the opportunities for growth that setbacks present.

Example: A student who fails an exam uses the experience as motivation to improve their study habits and seek additional help from teachers or tutors. They view the failure as an opportunity to develop better learning strategies.

2. Practice self-compassion: Be kind and supportive to yourself when faced with setbacks. Recognize that setbacks are a natural part of the learning process and treat yourself with understanding and forgiveness.

Example: A musician who struggles with a particularly challenging piece of music practices self-compassion by acknowledging that everyone has difficulties and that learning takes time. They avoid harsh self-criticism and focus on steady progress.

3. Seek support and guidance: Reach out to mentors coaches or peers who can provide guidance support and encouragement when facing setbacks. Learning from others' experiences can help you overcome obstacles more effectively.

Example: A new entrepreneur facing business challenges seeks guidance from a mentor or joins a business networking group to gain insights and support from experienced entrepreneurs who have overcome similar setbacks.

4. Adapt and adjust: Stay flexible and open to change during the learning process. Recognize that strategies may need to be adjusted or modified along the way to overcome obstacles effectively.

Example: A chef trying to master a new cooking technique experiments with different variations adjusts ingredients and seeks feedback to refine their skills. They adapt their approach based on the feedback received ultimately improving their technique.

5. Celebrate progress and small victories: Acknowledge and appreciate the progress you make no matter how small. Celebrating milestones and achievements boosts motivation increases self-confidence and fuels continued learning.

Example: An artist learning to paint recognizes improvements in their technique and accuracy. They celebrate completing their first portrait even if it may not be perfect and use it as motivation to continue refining their skills.

6. Maintain a growth mindset in the face of setbacks: Remember that setbacks are temporary and can be overcome with perseverance and a positive attitude. Focus on the long-term goal and maintain confidence in your ability to learn and grow.

Example: A project manager faces project delays and unforeseen challenges. Instead of viewing it as a failure they approach the situation with a growth mindset seeking solutions learning from the setbacks and adjusting project strategies to ensure success in the long run.

By adopting these strategies and embracing a resilient learning process individuals can navigate setbacks overcome obstacles and continue their journey towards lifelong success and personal fulfillment.

In conclusion learning for lifelong success requires the cultivation of a growth mindset the adoption of strategies for continuous learning and personal development and the embrace of a resilient learning process. By developing a growth mindset individuals can approach challenges with enthusiasm view failures as opportunities for growth and persist in the face of obstacles. Strategies for continuous learning and personal development involve setting clear goals creating learning plans utilizing diverse learning methods seeking feedback fostering learning communities and embracing technology and innovation. Overcoming setbacks and embracing a resilient learning process require adopting a growth mindset towards failure practicing self-compassion seeking support and guidance adapting and adjusting celebrating progress and maintaining a positive attitude. By incorporating these principles and practices into their lives individuals can embark on a lifelong journey of learning growth and personal success.

www.ingramcontent.com/pod-product-compliance
Lightning Source LLC
LaVergne TN
LVHW020441080526
838202LV00055B/5291